Sewing needles are amazing! The oldest needles recorded are from Russia and date to 30,000 BC. These bone needles look similar to the hand needles we use today. While it appears to be a simple little piece of metal, centuries of engineering and research have gone into designing the modern needle allowing us to stitch with ease by hand or machine.

Each hand and machine needle is designed for a specific purpose. Once you understand the differences in needles, you will be able to choose the correct needle for your stitch project to ensure stitching success.

Where to Find It

Printed in China
Copyright© 2014 by Landauer Publishing, LLC

Most frequently asked questions about sewing machine needles—

Does brand matter?
Generally, sewing machine needle brands are interchangeable so needles produced by any manufacturer will work. The exception to the interchangeable rule is the Schmetz and Organ brands. Schmetz needles are designed for sewing machines engineered and manufactured in Europe. Organ needles are designed for machines engineered and manufactured in Asia. If you are having stitch quality problems try switching needle brands.

What does a handicap designation on sewing machine needles mean?
Needles with a handicap designation have a slip-in threading system close to the eye to make it easier to thread.

How are sewing machine needles sized?
There are numbers listed on needle packages that indicate size. For sewing machine needles it is important to remember that the smaller the number the smaller the needle.

Why are there two sizes listed on machine needles?
The two sizes reflect the American and European sizing system. The American system ranges from size 8 to 19; the European system from size 60 to 120. The smaller numbers (8 and 60) designate small fine needles. Sewing machine needle size increases with larger numbers. The European system is based on the diameter of the needle blade in hundredths of a millimeter measured above the scarf or the short groove. A sewing machine needle with a blade diameter of 0.80 mm is written as NM (numeric metric) 80.

How do I choose the right size needle?
Choose the smallest needle that will easily accommodate the thread you are using, but make sure the needle is strong enough to stitch through your fabrics. The best way to discover the right size needle is to do some practice stitching on fabric scraps. This will help you determine if the needle, thread and fabric will work together.

2

Parts of a Sewing Machine Needle

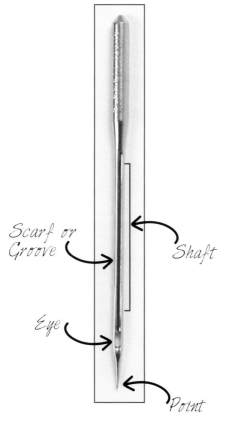

Scarf or Groove

Shaft

Eye

Point

3

Universal Needles

The Universal needle is a general use needle designed to find its way between a fabric's warp and weft threads rather than punching its way through.

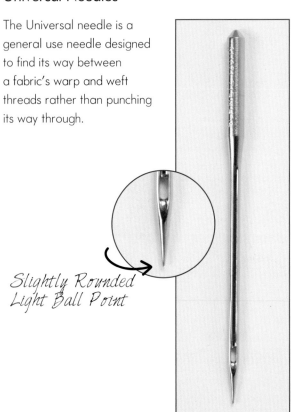

Slightly Rounded Light Ball Point

Sewing Machine Needles

Universal Needle Characteristics
• slightly rounded light ball point

Fabrics
• homespun and flannel
• linen
• osnaburg
• batiste
• scrim
• harem cloth
• hemp
• burlap
• cotton voile
• gauze
• crinoline
• knits
• jersey

Threads
• most fibers and weights

Sizes
• 60-120 (European)
• 8-19 (US)

Reminder: For sewing machine needles, the smaller the number the smaller the needle.

Tasks
• general sewing
• zigzag stitching

Note: Due to its rounded point, the universal needle is not ideal for sewing through tightly woven fabrics. Use a sharps needle instead.

Microtex/Sharps Needles

Microtex needles are excellent for stitch tasks in which precision, fine detailed stitching and perfectly straight stitches and lines are required.

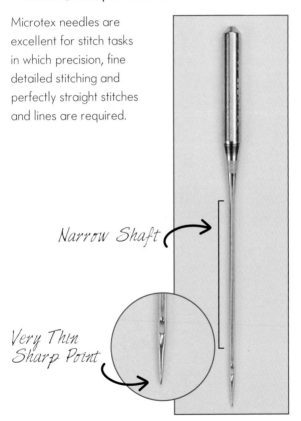

Narrow Shaft

Very Thin Sharp Point

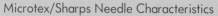

Sewing Machine Needles

Microtex/Sharps Needle Characteristics
- narrow shaft to allow for fine detailed stitching
- very thin sharp point

Fabrics
- cotton batik
- cotton lawn
- silk dupioni
- silk organza
- silk satin
- taffeta
- acetate
- brocade
- velvet
- faux suede
- artificial leathers
- Ripstop nylon
- Cordura®
- Gore-Tex®
- laminate coated fabrics
- microfibers

Sizes
- 60-110 (European)
- 8-18 (US)

Reminder: For sewing machine needles, the smaller the number the smaller the needle.

Tasks
- quilting
- heirloom stitch
- topstitching
- pintucks
- edge stitching

Threads
- most fibers and weights

Quilting Needles

Quilting needles are designed to stitch through thick layers and intersecting seams.

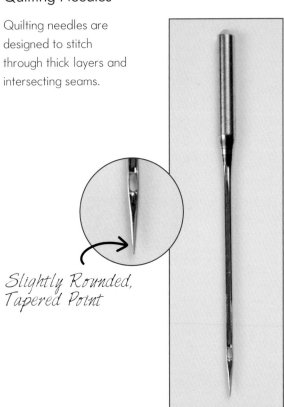

Slightly Rounded, Tapered Point

Sewing Machine Needles

Quilting Needle Characteristics
• slightly rounded and tapered point

Fabrics
• cotton

Sizes
• 75-90 (European)
• 11-14 (US)

Reminder: For sewing machine needles, the smaller the number the smaller the needle.

Note: When quilting batik fabrics consider using a Microtex needle. When micro-quilting with fine threads consider using a size 75 Embroidery or 60 Microtex needle.

Tasks
• general quilting with the feed dogs up
• stitching through multiple layers of fabric
• piecing cotton fabrics
• stitching through layers of fabric and batting or felt linings

Threads
• most fibers and weights

Embroidery Needles

Embroidery needles are designed to stitch in many directions making them the perfect choice for free motion quilting. They also allow you to stack the stitches close together without causing damage to the threads next to them.

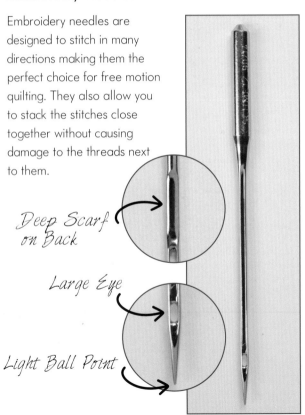

Deep Scarf on Back

Large Eye

Light Ball Point

Embroidery Needle Characteristics
- light ball point
- deeper scarf on back to help with loop formation with fine threads
- larger eye to reduce friction when using specialty and heavy weight threads

Fabrics
- all fabric types

Sizes
- 75-90 (European)
- 11-14 (US)

Reminder: For sewing machine needles, the smaller the number the smaller the needle.

Threads
- cotton
- rayon
- polyester
- metallic
- mylar
- linen
- wool

Tasks
- programmed embroidery
- free motion embroidery
- thread painting
- free motion quilting
- appliqué

Topstitch Needles

Topstitch needles are designed to stitch through heavy fabric or multiple layers. These needles will stitch perfectly straight lines through layers of fabric.

Large Shaft

Deep Groove

Long Eye

Very Short Point

Topstitch Needle Characteristics
- large shaft to reduce flex and allow very straight stitches
- very sharp point to aid in obtaining a straight line
- very long eye and deeper groove for heavier threads or to accommodate two threads at once

Fabrics
- medium- to heavy-weight
- mulitple layers

Sizes
- 80-100 (European)
- 12-16 (US)

Reminder: For sewing machine needles, the smaller the number the smaller the needle.

Tasks
- multiple fabric layer stitching
- straight stitching

Note: If you are topstitching on light-weight fabrics use a Microtex 60-70 size needle.

Threads
- most fibers and weights

Sewing Machine Needles

Jeans Needles

Jeans needles are designed to provide a consistent stitch when sewing through densely woven materials.

Thick Strong Shaft

Very Sharp Point

14

Jeans Needle Characteristics
• thick strong shaft
• very sharp point

Fabrics
• denim
• canvas
• heavy upholstery fabric
• imitation leather

Sizes
• 70-110 (European)
• 10-18 (US)

Reminder: For sewing machine needles, the smaller the number the smaller the needle.

Tasks
• consistent stitches through heavy layers or densely woven materials

Threads
• most fibers and weights

Metallic Needles

Metallic needles are designed specifically for use with metallic threads.

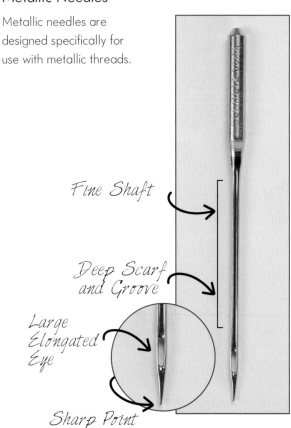

Fine Shaft

Deep Scarf and Groove

Large Elongated Eye

Sharp Point

Sewing Machine Needles

Metallic Needle Characteristics
- fine shaft
- larger elongated eye than an embroidery needle
- sharp point to reduce thread friction
- deep scarf and groove to accommodate wear of metal in thread

Fabrics
- wide range of light- to medium-weight

Sizes
- 80-90 (European)
- 12-14 (US)

Reminder: For sewing machine needles, the smaller the number the smaller the needle.

Tasks
- consistent stitches through heavy layers or densely woven materials

Note: If you prefer not to use a metallic needle when you are free motion stitching, try an embroidery needle. When you are using your machine's programmed stitches use a topstitch needle.

Threads
- metallic

Note: The metal in metallic threads can wear a groove in the needle itself so the needle may need to be changed more frequently.

Ball Point Needles

Ball Point needles are designed to ease between the threads of knit fabrics to avoid piercing and damaging them.

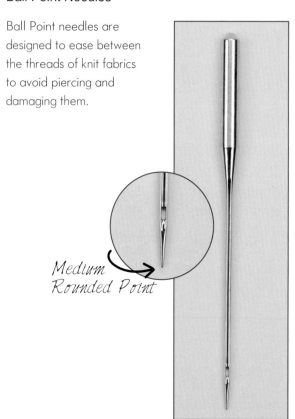

Medium Rounded Point

Sewing Machine Needles

Ball Point Needle Characteristics
• medium rounded point

Fabrics
• fine, lightweight knit
• silk jersey
• faux suede
• Spandex
• Tricot
• Lycra®
• swimsuit materials

Sizes
• 75-90 (European)
• 11-14 (US)

Reminder: For sewing machine needles, the smaller the number the smaller the needle.

Tasks
• stitch without piercing threads and damaging them
• smooth consistent stitches on knit or stretchy fabrics

Threads
• most fibers and weights

Stretch Needles

Stretch needles have a
rounded point and deep scarf
to prevent skipped stitches.

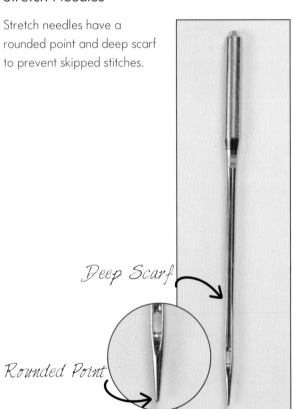

Deep Scarf

Rounded Point

Stretch Needle Characteristics
- rounded point
- deep scarf to prevent skipped stitches

Fabrics
- fine, lightweight knit
- silk jersey
- faux suede
- Spandex
- Tricot
- Lycra®
- swimsuit materials

Sizes
- 75-90 (European)
- 11-14 (US)

Reminder: For sewing machine needles, the smaller the number the smaller the needle.

Tasks
- stitch without skipping stitches
- smooth consistent stitches on knit or stretchy fabrics

Threads
- most fibers and weights

Twin Needles

Twin needles, or double needles, have two needles mounted on one shaft. When determining needle size, two numbers are listed. The first is the distance in millimeters between the needles and the second is the European needle size.

Two Needles Mounted on One Shaft

Twin Needle Characteristics
- two needles mounted on one shaft
- available in embroidery, denim, metallic and stretch

Sizes
- The project or fabric you are working on will determine what type and size twin needle to use. Check your sewing machine manual for specific information on sewing with a twin needle.

Tasks
- stitching light- to medium weight fabrics
- decorative stitching

Triple Needles

Triple needles, or drilling needles, have three needles mounted on one shaft. When determining needle size, two numbers are listed. The first is the distance in millimeters between the needles and the second is the European needle size.

Three Needles Mounted on One Shaft

Triple Needle Characteristics
- three needles mounted on one shaft
- available in universal

Sizes
- The project or fabric you are working on will determine what type and size triple needle to use. Check your sewing machine manual for specific information on sewing with a triple needle.

Tasks
- stitching light- to medium weight fabrics
- decorative topstitching

Specialty

Hemstitch Needles

Hemstitch needles have a flared shaft that looks like wings. This unique shape creates a decorative hole in tightly woven fabrics, fine batiste and linen.

Hemstitch (wing) Needle Characteristics
• flared shaft

Sizes
• 100-120

Tasks
• decorative stitching
• heirloom stitching
• hemstitching
• openwork

Double Hemstitch Needle Characteristics
• pairs a single hemstitch (wing) needle and universal needle together

Sizes
• 100

Tasks
• decorative stitching
• heirloom stitching

Specialty
Gold or Titanium Needles

These needles feature a Titanium Nitride coating. The titanium coating improves needle wear and resists burrs so needles last 5 to 7 times longer than uncoated needles. The coating does not make them stronger.

Large Eye
Slightly Rounded Point

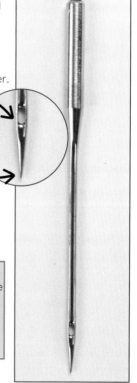

Gold/Titanium Needle Characteristics
- large eye
- slightly rounded point
- available in embroidery, topstitch and universal

Sizes
- 75-90 (European)
- 11-14 (US)

Reminder: For sewing machine needles, the smaller the number the smaller the needle.

Tasks
- stitching coarse or densely woven fabrics
- stitching batiks
- embroidery

25

Hand Sewing Needles

Most frequently asked questions about hand sewing needles—

Does brand matter?
There are many brands of hand sewing needles and it can get very confusing. While most hand stitchers have a preferred brand of needle, it is actually more important to make sure you are using the correct type and size needle for the job. Experiment with different needle brands to find one you prefer.

Most sewing needles are nickel-plated. If you have nickel allergies, try the Tulip brand piecing, quilting, appliqué, basting, leather and milliner's needles. These are specially polished and not nickel-plated.

How are hand sewing needles sized?
There are numbers listed on needle packages that indicate size. For hand sewing needles it is important to remember that the smaller the number the larger the needle.

How do I choose the right size needle?
Choose the smallest needle that will easily accommodate the thread you are using, but make sure the needle is strong and large enough to stitch through your fabrics.

The best way to discover the right size needle is by experimenting. What works for your friends may not work for you.

Parts of a Hand Sewing Needle

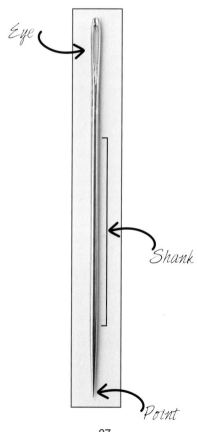

Eye

Shank

Point

Sharps Needles

Sharps needles are medium length with a round eye and a sharp point. It is the most commonly used needle.

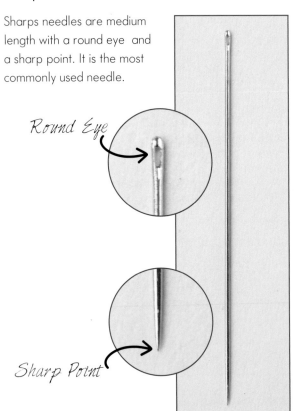

Round Eye

Sharp Point

Hand Sewing Needles

Sharps Needle Characteristics
- medium length
- round eye
- sharp point

Fabrics
smaller size needles
- fine, lightweight using smaller stitches

larger size needles
- medium- to heavy-weight

Sizes
- 1-12

Reminder: For hand sewing needles, the smaller the number the larger the needle.

Tasks
- general hand sewing
- hand piecing
- appliqué
- beading using size 10-12 needles

Threads
- light- to heavy-weight
- rayon
- polyester
- metallic
- mylar

Ball Point Needles

Ball Point needles have a rounded point and are designed to slip between the warp and weft threads rather than piercing them.

Round Point

Ball Point Needle Characteristics
• round point

Fabrics
• knits

Sizes
• 5-10

Reminder: For hand sewing needles, the smaller the number the larger the needle.

Tasks
• stitch between warp and weft threads without piercing them

Threads
• light- to medium-weight
• cotton
• rayon
• polyester

Embroidery Needles

Embroidery needles are also known as crewel needles. They have a sharp point and a large eye to accommodate thicker threads.

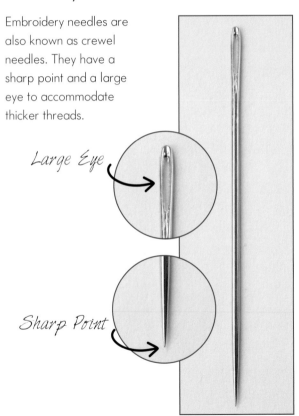

Large Eye

Sharp Point

Embroidery (Crewel) Needle Characteristics
• large eye to accommodate thicker threads
• sharp point

Fabrics
• all light- to medium-weight fabrics

Sizes
• 1-10

Reminder: For hand sewing needles, the smaller the number the larger the needle.

Tasks
• surface embroidery
• crewel work
• use in place of a sharps needle if the sharps is difficult to thread

Threads
• pearl cotton
• multiple strands of embroidery floss
• thick

33

Quilting Needles

Quilting needles are also known as betweens. They are shorter than sharps needles giving a quilter more control when stitching.

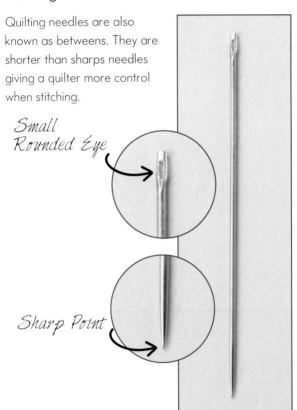

Small Rounded Eye

Sharp Point

Hand Sewing Needles

Quilting Needle (Betweens) Characteristics
- shorter length than sharps
- small rounded eye
- sharp point

Fabrics
- cottons
- cotton blends

Sizes
- 1-12

Reminder: For hand sewing needles, the smaller the number the larger the needle.

Tasks
- hand quilting
- stacking multiple small stitches onto the needle before pulling it through the quilt layers

Threads
- light- to medium-weight
- cotton
- rayon
- linen
- polyester

Milliner's Needles

Milliner's needles are also known as straw needles. They are very long and were engineered for the Milliner's (hat) making industry.

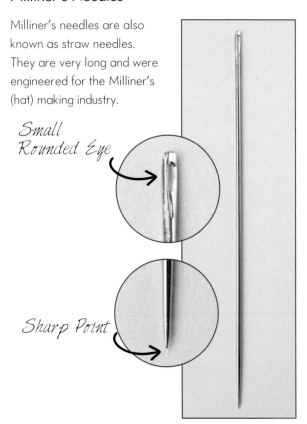

Small Rounded Eye

Sharp Point

36

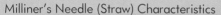

Milliner's Needle (Straw) Characteristics
- very long
- small round eye
- sharp point

Fabrics
- light-weight such as sheers, silks, chiffons
- medium-weight such as quilting cottons, batiks, muslin

Sizes
- 5-10

Reminder: For hand sewing needles, the smaller the number the larger the needle.

Tasks
- basting
- pleating
- smocking
- decorative stitches
- beading
- large-scale appliqué

Threads
- ultra-fine
- fine
- medium-weight
- cotton
- rayon
- polyester

Not suitable for heavy threads

Appliqué Needles

Appliqué needles are very similar to sharps, but have a thinner, longer shaft that is better suited for fine appliqué techniques. For larger scale appliqué work, a milliner's needle may work best.

Rounded Eye

Sharp Point

Appliqué Needle Characteristics
- round eye
- sharp point
- medium length

Fabrics
smaller needles (11-12)
- sheers
- chiffons

larger needles (9-10)
- cotton
- linen
- wool

Sizes
- 9-12

Reminder: For hand sewing needles, the smaller the number the larger the needle.

Tasks
- appliqué
- binding
- beading
- fine hemming

Threads
- ultra-fine
- fine
- medium-weight
- cotton
- rayon
- polyester

Not suitable for heavy threads

Sashiko Needles

Sashiko needles are longer and thicker than other needles. They are similar to a chenille needle, but the shaft is straight rather than tapered. Sashiko needles are extra long to allow many stacked stitches on the shaft before pulling the thread through, resulting in straighter stitches.

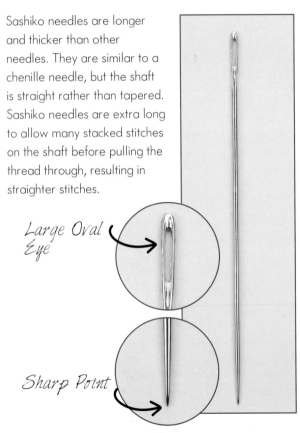

Large Oval Eye

Sharp Point

40

Sashiko Needle Characteristics
- long straight shaft
- large oval eye
- sharp point

Fabrics
- loosely woven fabrics
- linen
- cotton
- sashiko cloth

Sizes
- range of sizes from short (1.68") to long (2.75")

Tasks
- sashiko stitching
- running stitch basting
- embroidery

Threads
- sashiko
- embroidery floss
- pearl cotton

Tapestry Needles

Tapestry needles have a blunt point which is designed to go between the warp and weft of loosely woven fabrics. The large eye is perfect for the thick threads and yarns in embroidery.

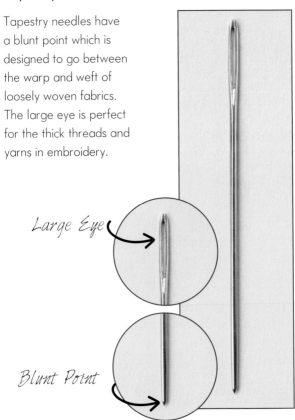

Large Eye

Blunt Point

Hand Sewing Needles

Tapestry Needle Characteristics
- large eye
- blunt point
- tapered shaft

Fabrics
- linen
- felt
- needlepoint canvas
- Aida
- plastic canvas
- loosely woven

Sizes
- 13-28

Reminder: For hand sewing needles, the smaller the number the larger the needle.

Tasks
- cross stitch
- needlepoint
- embroidery
- bookbinding

Threads
- heavy-weight
- yarn
- embroidery floss
- pearl cotton
- embroidery threads
- silk ribbon

43

Chenille Needles

Chenille needles have a sharp point and large eye to accommodate heavy threads and yarns.

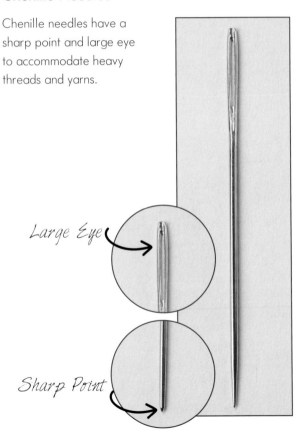

Large Eye

Sharp Point

44

Hand Sewing Needles

Chenille Needle Characteristics
- large eye
- sharp point
- tapered shaft

Fabrics
- heavy-weight
- tightly woven
- felt
- canvas
- duck cloth

Sizes
- 13-26

Reminder: For hand sewing needles, the smaller the number the larger the needle.

Tasks
- crewel
- ribbonwork
- general embroidery
- bookbinding

Threads
- embroidery floss
- pearl cotton
- embroidery threads
- silk ribbon
- heavy-weight
- yarn

45

Beading Needles

Beading needles are long fine needles with an oval eye. They are designed to easily go through the small holes in beads. The longer length allows many beads to be picked up at once.

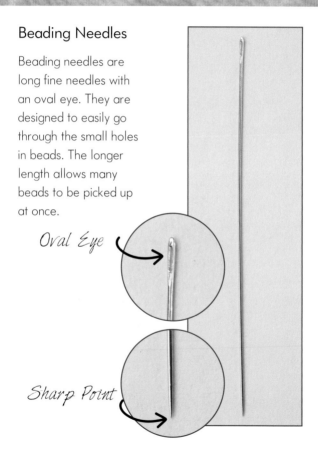

Oval Eye

Sharp Point

Beading Needle Characteristics
• oval eye
• sharp point

Note: Since beading needles are thin, they are easily bent when stitching through fabric. However, this should not alter the outcome of your beading.

Fabrics
• all types from light-weight silk to tightly woven canvas

Sizes
• 10-15

Reminder: For hand sewing needles, the smaller the number the larger the needle.

Tasks
• loom beading
• beading on fabric

Threads
• beading

Darner Needles

Darner needles are long needles with a long oval eye. This makes them useful for darning, mending and basting layers of fabrics together.

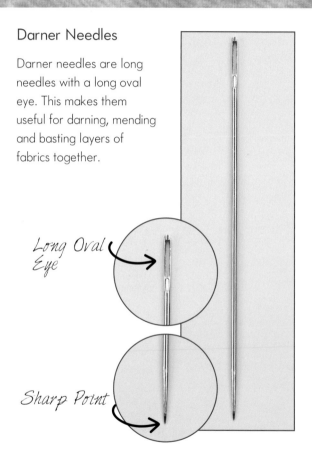

Long Oval Eye

Sharp Point

Darner Needle Characteristics
- long
- long oval eye
- sharp point

Fabrics
- all types
- knitted items

Sizes
Darners are available in a variety of sizes for different jobs

- 5-9 (cotton)
- 1-9 (long)
- 14-18 (yarn)

Reminder: For hand sewing needles, the smaller the number the larger the needle.

Tasks
- smocking
- embroidery
- darning/mending
- ribbon embroidery
- sewing knitting or crochet together
- basting layers of fabric together
- soft sculpture
- home décor

Threads
- medium- to heavy-weight
- embroidery floss
- pearl cotton

Specialty

Doll Needles

Doll needles are also
known as soft sculpture
needles. These are
extra long thin needles
with long oval eyes for
soft sculpting and molding
of doll features.

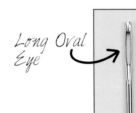

*Long Oval
Eye*

Doll Needle Characteristics
- extra long and thin
- long oval eye
- sharp point

Tasks
- soft sculpting
  and molding
  doll features
- needle sculpting
  doll faces
- tying quilts

Sizes
- 3"-9" long

Reminder:
For hand sewing
needles, the smaller
the number the
larger the needle.

Sharp Point

Specialty

Bodkin Needles

Bodkin needles are thick long needles with a ball point end and large oval eye. These needles are not designed for sewing but rather to pull trims or elastic through casings and slits in fabric.

Long Oval Eye

Ball Point Rounded Tip

Bodkin Needle Characteristics
• long and thick
• long oval eye
• rounded point

Tasks
• pull elastic through casing
• weave flat trims and ribbons through lace openings or fabric slits

Sizes
• available in small and large

Specialty

Leather Needles

Leather needles are also known as glovers. They have a sharp triangular point to pierce leather and similar fabrics without tearing them.

Small Eye

Leather Needle Characteristics
• sharp triangular point

Tasks
• pierce through leather, suede, vinyl or plastic without tearing them

Sizes
• 3-7

Reminder:
For hand sewing needles, the smaller the number the larger the needle.

Sharp Triangular Point

Hand Sewing Needles

Specialty

Double Eye Needles

Double eye needles are available with a blunt or sharp point. These needles allow you to use two threads in different colors without changing to a larger needle. This unique design feature minimizes friction that often occurs when using multiple thicker threads.

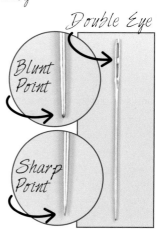

Double Eye

Blunt Point

Sharp Point

Double Eye Needle Characteristics
• sharp or blunt point
• two eyes

Fabrics
• blunt point
  - loosely woven fabrics such as canvas, linen, wool, muslin and flannel
• sharp point
  - tightly woven fabrics such as cotton, batiks and silks

Sizes
• 15-24

Reminder:
For hand sewing needles, the smaller the number the larger the needle.

Threads
• most fibers and weights
• silk ribbon may be used in larger size needles

Specialty

Carpet Sharps Needles

Carpet Sharps needles are basically larger versions of the sharps needle.

Round Eye

Carpet Sharps Needle Characteristics
- longer and thicker than a sharps needle
- round eye
- sharp point

Tasks
- rug and carpet design
- any heavy duty sewing task such as home décor, camping equipment and backpacks

Sizes
- 16-18

Reminder: For hand sewing needles, the smaller the number the larger the needle.

Sharp Point

Hand Sewing Needles

Specialty

Upholstery Needles

Upholstery needles are large long needles that can be straight or curved.

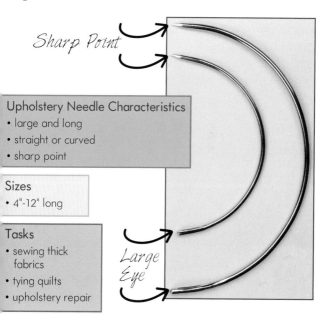

Sharp Point

Large Eye

Upholstery Needle Characteristics
- large and long
- straight or curved
- sharp point

Sizes
- 4"-12" long

Tasks
- sewing thick fabrics
- tying quilts
- upholstery repair

Thank You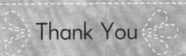

Many thanks to all the needle manufacturers who provide us with amazing tiny tools that allow us to stitch whatever our creative souls can imagine. Special thanks to Clover and Schmetz for providing the needles photographed in this book.

For more information about Liz Kettle visit www.textileevolution.com

For more information or to order:
Landauer Publishing
1-800-557-2144 or landauerpub.com